UNSOLVED HISTORICAL MYSTERIES

by Allison Lassieur

Consultant:
Tim Solie
Adjunct Professor of History
Minnesota State University, Mankato

CAPSTONE PRESS
a capstone imprint

Edge Books are published by Capstone Press,
1710 Roe Crest Drive, North Mankato, Minnesota 56003
www.capstonepub.com

Library of Congress Cataloging-in-Publication Data
Lassieur, Allison.
Unsolved historical mysteries / by Allison Lassieur.
pages cm.—(Edge books. Unsolved mystery files)
Summary: "Describes mysterious and unsolved historical events from
around the world"—Provided by publisher.
Includes bibliographical references and index.
ISBN 978-1-4914-4264-7 (library binding)
ISBN 978-1-4914-4340-8 (paperback)
ISBN 978-1-4914-4320-0 (ebook PDF)
1. History—Miscellanea—Juvenile literature. 2. Curiosities and
wonders—Juvenile literature. I. Title.
D10.L365 2016
909—dc23   2015001432

Editorial Credits
Aaron Sautter, editor; Sarah Bennett, designer; Gina Kammer,
media researcher; Morgan Walters, production specialist

Photo Credits
Alamy: © John Morrison, 21, © Mary Evans Picture Library, 7, © Robert Estall photo agency, 18;
Corbis: National Geographic Creative/© Keenpress, 23; Getty Images: De Agostini Picture Library,
11, Sovfoto, 23; Granger, NYC: 27; Shutterstock: American Spirit, 29, Antlio, (background) 16-17,
19, Claire McAdams, (fog smoky background) throughout, djgis, 10-11, Janece Flippo, 15, Jon
Bilous, (background) 12-13, Mark Heider, (Earth map) throughout, Milosz_G, (background) 22-23,
24-25, MisterElements, (ink splatters) throughout, Roobcio, (grunge background) throughout,
seahorsetwo, 4, Steve Heap, (background) 18, TAGSTOCK1, cover, 16-17, Ursa Major, (worn
background) throughout; Wikimedia: 13, 14, (inset) 21, Beinecke Rare Book & Manuscript Library,
Yale University, 6-7, 8, 9

Printed in China by Nordica
0415/CA21500562
042015   008844NORDF15

Contents

Mysteries
That Time
Can't Solve

Secret codes that no one can solve. People who disappear forever. Treasures that vanish without a trace. These historical mysteries and others have stumped people for hundreds or even thousands of years.

How can these mysteries go unsolved for so long? Sometimes facts get lost or forgotten. Records are often destroyed. People who may know things die. And sometimes no one cares about the mystery when it happens. It is only later that someone wonders what happened and tries to solve the mystery.

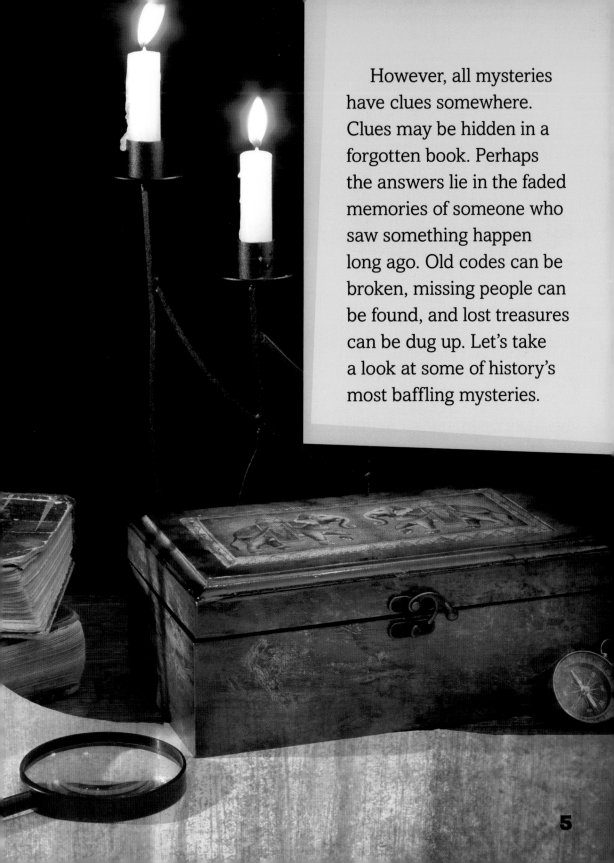

However, all mysteries have clues somewhere. Clues may be hidden in a forgotten book. Perhaps the answers lie in the faded memories of someone who saw something happen long ago. Old codes can be broken, missing people can be found, and lost treasures can be dug up. Let's take a look at some of history's most baffling mysteries.

The Book That Can't Be Read

Hidden among rare books in Yale University's library is one of the world's biggest unsolved mysteries. Most people don't even know it's there. Those who do know about it don't know how to read it. It's called the Voynich **manuscript**—a strange old book that no one has ever been able to read or understand.

Almost nothing is known about the book's origins. It was written more than 500 years ago in the 1400s, and it was probably made in Italy. But nobody knows who wrote it or why.

This mysterious book looks similar to other **medieval** books of the time period. It's filled with drawings of plants, the night sky, and beautiful looping handwriting. But take a closer look and things start to get strange. The drawings of plants are of no known plants on Earth. The text is also written in a bizarre, unknown language.

Wilfrid Voynich researched and collected many
rare books across Europe during the early 1900s.

Rare book collector Wilfrid Voynich
discovered this strange book in 1912.
He found it while looking through a
collection of other old books at a castle
in Italy. Voynich tried to crack the
manuscript's code, but failed. For nearly
100 years, expert **cryptographers** have
tried to unlock the book's secrets. But
nobody has been able to figure it out.

manuscript—a document, such as a book or an article

medieval—having to do with the period of European
history between AD 500 and 1450

cryptographer—a person who makes and breaks codes

What's It About?

If someone were to crack the manuscript's code, what would they learn? Experts have guessed that the book might be a scientific work written in a forgotten language. Some people think the book is filled with secret knowledge written in an unknown ancient code. But others feel the Voynich manuscript is just an impressive fake. They think someone created it to fool the world into thinking he or she was an experienced doctor. But until the book's secrets can be revealed, no one will know the truth.

Clues to Cracking the Voynich Code

Professor Stephen Bax is a language professor at the University of Bedfordshire in England. Like everyone else, the Voynich manuscript perplexed him until he got an idea. He began looking for proper names listed next to the manuscript's strange pictures. He then compared the names to other old manuscripts and ancient languages. Bax soon began recognizing some words. He managed to decode the name Taurus next to a group of star drawings. He also identified several plant names scattered through the text. Bax hopes to one day translate the whole manuscript and solve the mystery for good.

The Voynich manuscript's drawings of strange plants, diagrams, and star charts have baffled researchers for many years.

The Ship That Went Nowhere

Most ghost ships are not the spooky kind said to be haunted by ghosts or spirits. Instead, like ghost towns, most ghost ships are vessels that have been deserted. Crew members and passengers seem to simply vanish without a trace. On December 4, 1872, Captain David Moorehouse found one of these ghost ships. He was sailing between the Azores islands and Portugal when his crew spotted a ship drifting on the waves. They had found the *Mary Celeste*, which had sailed from New York eight days before. It had carried Captain Briggs, his wife and child, and seven crewmen.

But something was wrong. Nobody was onboard. Captain Moorehouse knew the *Mary Celeste* was supposed to be in Italy. He ordered his crew to investigate the ship. They found it to be in good shape. The crew's belongings were still in place. The cargo still sat intact. And there was plenty of food and water. However, the ship's lifeboat and **navigation** equipment were missing. It was clear that everyone had abandoned ship. But what made them leave behind a seaworthy ship filled with supplies?

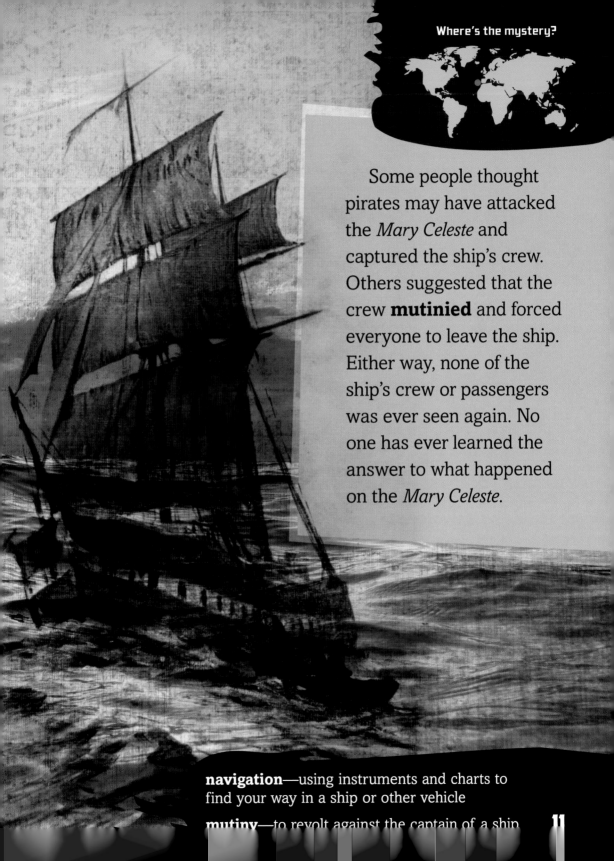

Some people thought pirates may have attacked the *Mary Celeste* and captured the ship's crew. Others suggested that the crew **mutinied** and forced everyone to leave the ship. Either way, none of the ship's crew or passengers was ever seen again. No one has ever learned the answer to what happened on the *Mary Celeste*.

navigation—using instruments and charts to find your way in a ship or other vehicle

mutiny—to revolt against the captain of a ship

The Mysterious Treasure Map

Somewhere under the green hills of Virginia, a huge treasure is rumored to lie hidden. Only one clue about the treasure exists: a written message in three parts. However, it was written in a secret code that no one has ever completely broken.

The mysterious story began in 1885 with a **pamphlet** published in Virginia. It told the remarkable story of Thomas Beale. He had supposedly made a fortune mining gold and silver in the Wild West in the 1820s. According to the story, Beale later buried his huge treasure in Bedford County, Virginia. To keep its location safe he created three messages in coded **ciphers**. One message is thought to explain where the treasure was hidden. The second supposedly describes how much treasure there was. The third is believed to be a list of Beale's fellow miners and their families. Beale then locked the messages in an iron box and gave it to his trusted friend, Robert Morriss, before leaving for St. Louis.

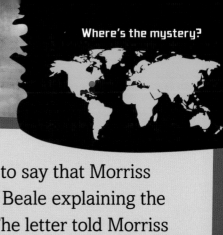

The story goes on to say that Morriss later got a letter from Beale explaining the mysterious ciphers. The letter told Morriss to wait 10 years before opening the box. In the meantime, Beale would send another letter with the key to the codes.

The Beale ciphers were made up of a series of seemingly random numbers.

71, 194, 38, 1701, 89, 76, 11, 83, 1629, 48, 94, 63, 132, 16, 111, 95, 84, 341, 975,14, 40, 64, 27, 81, 139, 213, 63, 90, 1120, 918, 40, 74, 758, 485,604, 230, 436, 664, 582, 124, 211, 486, 225, 401, 370,11, 101, 98, 193, 145, 1, 94, 73, 416, 918, 36, 219, 27, 176, 130, 10, 460, 25, 3,118, 320, 138, 36, 416, 280, 15, 88, 61, 304, 12, 21,24, 283, 134, 184, 360, 780, 18, 64, 463, 474, 4, 581, 34, 69, 128, 367, 460, 17, 03, 862, 70, 60, 1317, 471, 540, 9, 568 614, 1   19, 812,

pamphlet—a small booklet

cipher—a code that uses numbers or symbols to represent

The Mystery Grows Deeper

Unfortunately for Morriss, the second letter with the key never came. Beale had apparently disappeared. Nobody knew what happened to him, and Morriss never heard from him again.

In spite of this, Morriss kept his promise. He didn't open the box until 1845. But it made no difference. He spent years trying to decode the messages. After Morriss died the papers eventually fell into the hands of James Ward. Ward claimed to solve the second cipher, but couldn't figure out the others. Eventually he grew tired of the mystery and published the pamphlet. Treasure hunters have been trying to crack the code and find the treasure ever since.

Some people say the pamphlet was a **hoax** and that the ciphers can't be solved. They say that Thomas Beale wasn't even a real person, and that Ward made up the whole story. It's possible that the whole thing is a fake. With few solid clues, it seems no one will ever know the truth.

THE

BEALE PAPERS,

CONTAINING

AUTHENTIC STATEMENTS

REGARDING THE

TREASURE BURIED

IN

1819 AND 1821,

NEAR

BUFORDS, IN BEDFORD COUNTY, VIRGINIA,

AND

WHICH HAS NEVER BEEN RECOVERED.

PRICE FIFTY CENTS.

LYNCHBURG:
VIRGINIA BOOK AND JOB PRINT.
1885.

hoax—a trick to make people believe something that is not true

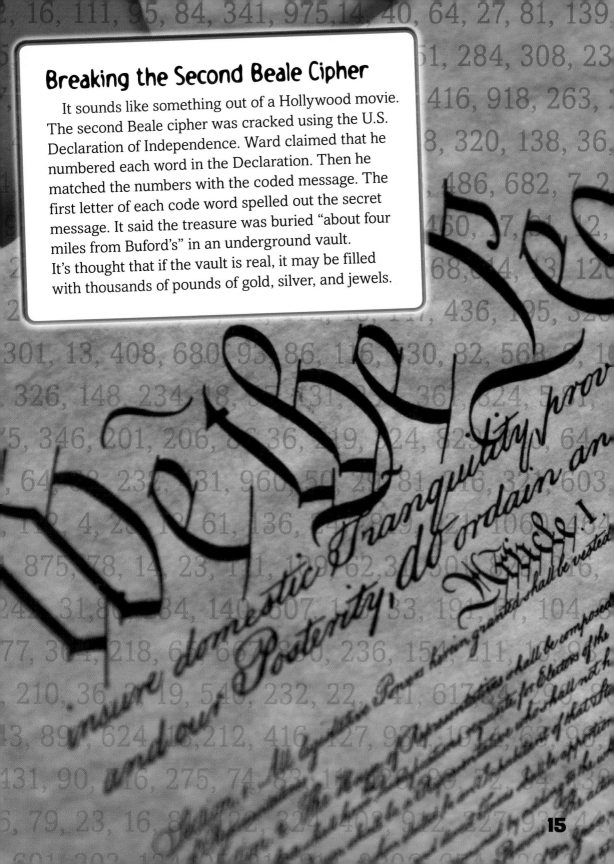

Breaking the Second Beale Cipher

It sounds like something out of a Hollywood movie. The second Beale cipher was cracked using the U.S. Declaration of Independence. Ward claimed that he numbered each word in the Declaration. Then he matched the numbers with the coded message. The first letter of each code word spelled out the secret message. It said the treasure was buried "about four miles from Buford's" in an underground vault.

It's thought that if the vault is real, it may be filled with thousands of pounds of gold, silver, and jewels.

The Green Children of Woolpit

In the mid-1100s wolves commonly roamed the dark and dangerous forests around Woolpit, England. Villagers often dug deep pits to trap the beasts, which gave the small town its name.

But one afternoon men working in the fields got a shock. They found two young children, a girl and a boy, in one of the wolf pits. The children's skin was a bright green color. They wore clothing made of materials that no one recognized. And they spoke a language no one could understand.

The farmers took the children to a local landowner, Sir Richard de Calne. He kindly offered them food and water, but the children burst into tears. They refused to eat anything other than raw green beans. The green children ate nothing but the beans for months until they became used to other food.

Slowly the green color faded from the children's skin. They also learned to speak some English and began telling people a fantastic story. They said they were a brother and sister from a strange place called St. Martin's Land. The sun never shined there. The light was always like twilight, and everything was green—even the people.

A banner in St. Mary's Church in Woolpit shows the story of the Green Children and the last sighting of wild wolves in England.

St MARY

WOOLPIT

Where Did They Come From?

The mysterious children said they had been herding their father's animals when they wandered into a cave. Inside the cave they heard bells. They followed the sound until they were blinded by bright sunlight. When they came out of the cave, the children found themselves stuck in the wolf pit.

Could this strange story be true? Did two green children just mysteriously appear out of nowhere? Many people think this tale is just a fantastic legend. However, there is evidence that the children were real. During that time two men researched the mystery and wrote down the stories people told about the green children. One of them even spoke with Sir Richard de Calne about his personal experience with the children.

If the green children were real, where did they come from? One idea states that they were **refugees** from another country who spoke a different language. But what could have caused the children's skin to be green? Some people think they may have been suffering from **malnutrition** or **arsenic** poisoning, which can turn the skin green. The truth about the green children is a mystery that may never be solved.

refugee—a person forced to flee his or her home because of natural disaster or war

malnutrition—a condition caused by a lack of healthy foods in a person's diet

arsenic—a poisonous chemical

19

The Holy Grail of Mysteries

Shugborough Hall, a grand mansion in Staffordshire, England, holds many secrets. But its biggest secret is not inside its 300-year-old walls. Hidden among the surrounding gardens stands a weatherworn stone monument. Look closely and you'll see a mysterious series of letters carved into the stone. Some people think the letters may be a clue to one of the biggest mysteries in the world—the lost **Holy Grail**.

The letters aren't the only part of the mystery. The image above the letters has secrets of its own. It is based on a painting by Nicolas Poussin, who was rumored to be a **Templar**. Members of the Templars were said to be the eternal guardians of the Holy Grail. Poussin is thought to have hidden clues about the Grail in his painting. Some people believe the coded letters and hidden clues are connected. They think that if this mystery was solved, the location of the Holy Grail would be discovered.

Holy Grail—the legendary cup or bowl that was believed to be used by Jesus Christ at the Last Supper

Templar—a knight of a secret religious military order

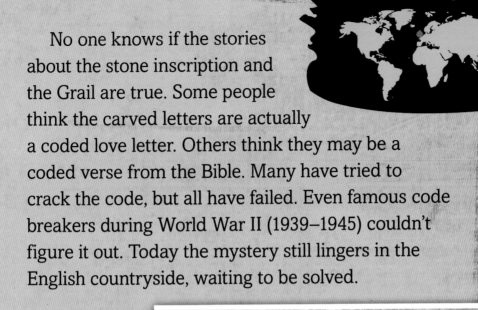

No one knows if the stories about the stone inscription and the Grail are true. Some people think the carved letters are actually a coded love letter. Others think they may be a coded verse from the Bible. Many have tried to crack the code, but all have failed. Even famous code breakers during World War II (1939–1945) couldn't figure it out. Today the mystery still lingers in the English countryside, waiting to be solved.

O·U·O·S·V·A·V·V

D·   M·

The Mystery of Missing Amber

It was once called "The Eighth Wonder of the World." Its extraordinary beauty stunned visitors to the Catherine Palace in St. Petersburg, Russia. This incredible treasure was called The **Amber** Room. It was covered with more than 6 tons (5.4 metric tons) of rich amber panels and semiprecious stones. People marveled at how the room "glowed a fiery gold" when all 565 candles were lit.

The Amber Room was the treasure of kings. It was first given to Russia's Peter the Great as a gift from the King of Prussia in 1716. It stayed in St. Petersburg until 1755 and was then moved to the Catherine Palace. However, the room's fate changed when World War II broke out and Germany invaded Russia.

amber—a yellow-brown substance formed from fossilized tree resin; amber is often used to make jewelry and other works of art

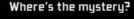

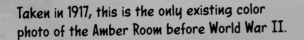

Taken in 1917, this is the only existing color photo of the Amber Room before World War II.

By then the Catherine Palace had become a museum. Its caretakers knew the Germans usually stole any art and treasure they could find. They frantically tried to move the amber panels to safety. Unfortunately, the panels were old and brittle and couldn't be moved easily. So the caretakers covered up the rich amber with wallpaper instead. But this didn't fool the German soldiers. They found the room, packed the precious panels into crates, and sent them to Konigsberg, Germany.

An Unknown Fate

For a time the Amber Room was installed at the Konigsberg castle museum. But the castle was bombed in 1944—destroying the treasured room in a fiery blaze.

But was it truly destroyed? In the chaos and destruction of war, it's possible the Amber Room survived after all. For the last 70 years treasure hunters and historians have tried to discover what really happened. Some witnesses swear the room was destroyed, but others claimed to see heavy crates at the railway station near the castle. It's possible that the crates held the amber panels and were buried in secret bunkers outside the city. Some people also thought the panels were loaded onto a ship, which then sank in the Baltic Sea.

Then in 1997 German police found one of the jeweled amber panels. Its owner had received it from his soldier father. He claimed he didn't know where the panel had come from, but the find encouraged treasure hunters to keep searching. Since then many have claimed to find the Amber Room. But all the reports have been wrong so far. The treasured room remains missing to this day.

A replica of the Amber Room was opened in the
Catherine Palace in St. Petersburg, Russia, in 2003.

The Mysterious Lost Colony

History is filled with many cases of missing people. These people are often found alive and well, but others aren't. Four hundred years ago, an entire **colony** of people disappeared—and their fate is still a mystery today.

In 1587 John White arrived in North America with 117 English men, women, and children. They hoped to build a settlement on Roanoke Island, just off the coast of present-day North Carolina. It was the second time British colonists tried to settle at Roanoke. Another small group had tried before but failed. However, White's group had more people and supplies. Surely they would survive.

Later that year White returned to England to get more supplies for the new settlement. But while he was there, war broke out between England and Spain. It was too dangerous for English ships to leave. White was forced to stay in England until 1590.

colony—a place that is settled by people from another country and is controlled by that country

The only solid clue to the fate of the Roanoke colony was the word "Croatoan" carved into a large fence post.

When he finally returned, the ship's crew blew trumpets to let the settlers know they had arrived. But nobody answered. It was strangely quiet. The houses had been taken down and the area was deserted. There were no bodies or other signs of attack. Where had everyone gone? There were only two clues: the word "Croatoan" carved into some wood, and the letters "Cro" carved into a tree.

All Are Lost

White wasn't very worried at first. Before he had left the colony, the settlers had agreed on a plan if something happened. They would get help from the Croatoans, an American Indian tribe near the Roanoke settlement.

White planned to search for the missing settlers among the Croatoan Indians. But before he could begin, a fierce storm hit the coast. White and his crew were forced to sail back to England. White died soon after he returned to England, never knowing what happened at Roanoke. A few search parties did return to look for the colonists, but the missing people were never found.

Where did the people go? Perhaps they joined the Croatoan people or one of the other tribes in the area. Maybe they were all kidnapped and killed. Or perhaps they died of disease—but no bodies were ever found. One theory says the colonists moved and rebuilt the settlement in another place. The fate of the Roanoke colony remains one of the most mysterious unsolved historical mysteries to this day.

Whether it's missing people, strangely coded documents, or lost treasures, many people are fascinated by history's puzzling mysteries. It's possible that these mysteries will never be solved. But historians will keep hunting for the clues that will lead them to the answers.

Glossary

amber (AM-buhr)—a yellow-brown substance formed from fossilized tree resin; amber is often used to make jewelry and other works of art

arsenic (AR-suh-nik)—a poisonous chemical

cipher (SY-fur)—a code that uses numbers or symbols to represent letters of the alphabet

colony (KAH-luh-nee)—a place that is settled by people from another country and is controlled by that country

cryptographer (KRYP-tah-gruh-fer)—a person who makes and breaks codes

hoax (HOHKS)—a trick to make people believe something that is not true

Holy Grail (HOH-lee GRAYL)—the legendary cup or bowl that was believed to be used by Jesus Christ at the Last Supper

malnutrition (mal-noo-TRISH-uhn)—a condition caused by a lack of healthy foods in a person's diet

manuscript (MAN-yoo-skript)—a handwritten document, such as a book or article

medieval (mee-DEE-vuhl)—having to do with the period of European history between AD 500 and 1450

mutiny (MYOOT-uh-nee)—a revolt against the captain of a ship

navigation (nav-uh-GAY-shuhn)—using instruments and charts to find your way in a ship or other vehicle

pamphlet (PAM-flet)—a small booklet

refugee (ref-yoo-JEE)—a person forced to flee his or her home because of natural disaster or war

Templar (TEMP-lahr)—a knight of a religious military order during the early 1100s

Read More

Levy, Janey. *Roanoke: The Lost Colony*. History's Mysteries. New York: Gareth Stevens Publishing, 2015.

Montgomerie, Adrienne. *Ghost Ships*. Mystery Files. New York: Crabtree Pub. Company, 2013.

Rice, Dona Herweck. *Unsolved! History's Mysteries*. Time for Kids Nonfiction Readers. Huntington Beach, Calif.: Teacher Created Materials, 2012.

Internet Sites

FactHound offers a safe, fun way to find Internet sites related to this book. All of the sites on FactHound have been researched by our staff.

Here's all you do:

Visit *www.facthound.com*

Type in this code: 9781491442647

Check out projects, games and lots more at
www.capstonekids.com

Index